"*Butterfly Nebula* is a rare creation of son̨ eco-consciousness, of emotional complexity̨ ......ness. In a world where empathy is under threat of erasure, these poems show us how 'dust become[s] the blood,' how the heart can be a 'universal symbol,' and how ours is inherently a 'liquid alphabet.' These poems take responsibility for themselves while reminding us of our own responsibilities to the world and each other. There's such sharpness to Hogan's metaphors, such richness to the world she builds for us, both defining and pushing against the edges of our shared human experience. 'It is said all flesh is grass' and 'that we are ashes / and to ashes we return,' but Hogan knows the truth, uncertain as it may always be to us. 'A prophet folded may appear to be dead,' but in the world of *Butterfly Nebula*, nothing is ever truly dead. These poems choose to both celebrate and mourn everything they touch. Even their own ghosts. Even that greater truth that always remains just slightly out of reach, that she refuses to stop reaching toward."

—**JOHN SIBLEY WILLIAMS**, author of *Skin Memory*

"Laura Reece Hogan's work is unforgettable because it's true, true the way Hopkins or Dickinson are true, who must bend words to tell the truth of what it feels like to be separate, all the while knowing there is more than separation to the story, more even to the stories than their beginnings and comings to an end. Hogan is one of the brilliant lights that only rarely comes along."

—**DAVID KEPLINGER**, author of *The World to Come*

"Beautiful. Months after reading these gorgeous poems, that word surfaces each time I think about *Butterfly Nebula*. Beautiful in its spiritual reach, beautiful in its often odd and always exquisite imagery, and beautiful in its composition, *Butterfly Nebula* lifts us into the galaxy in one line and plunges us into the ocean the next. Hogan's articulation of longing seduced me, her words voicing thoughts still vague in my heart. In 'Soul Nebula,' she writes: 'You wonder / why the inside must be swept clear // so violently, / the aching cavities carved // by radiation.' In the visionary tradition, she wrestles with life's spiritual contradictions and looks to nature for answers: 'the Elysia sea slug / sprouts a heart from just a head. This is your prescription.' Inspired by laws of physics, the lyrebird, Lazarus, by stingrays, saints, and supernovas, *Butterfly Nebula* offers communion for all seekers. These are poems of praise, and they praise in their poetry."

—**CHRISTINE STEWART-NUÑEZ**, author of *The Poet and the Architect*

"Laura Reece Hogan's *Butterfly Nebula* is a 'prayer . . . of the whole body, / of clamor and catastrophe, of take me and make me, of chaos / and clarity.' Hogan's words 'speak sky,' their gravitational pull irresistible. With poems that whirl us through space; propel us across continents; hurl us through time and its tales; then plunge us deep into sea, woods, body, and faith, the author redefines metamorphosis. Astronomical, biological, ecological, theological, metaphorical: these 'dark nebula[e]' are ours, 'cradling new stars.' How dazzling the shine of these poems, how far-reaching the trek of their light."

—**MARJORIE MADDOX**, author of *Begin with a Question*

"In *Butterfly Nebula* Laura Reece Hogan gives us poems that begin in acts of radical seeing and observation, and in these detailed, effulgent poems, we go with the poet as she looks through telescopes, or through microscopes, is at sea, or on land, and then names, notes, and describes the staggering complexity of our natural world. The poems in this captivating book commingle science and faith, and rather than seeing these two pillars of understanding as contradictory, *Butterfly Nebula* shows us—through the tensile mechanics of poetry—just how human curiosity brings us closer to the divine."

—**MARK WUNDERLICH**, author of *God of Nothingness*

The
Backwaters
Press

THE BACKWATERS PRIZE IN POETRY

Butterfly
Nebula

LAURA REECE HOGAN

THE BACKWATERS PRESS
An imprint of the University of Nebraska Press

Acknowledgments for the use of copyrighted material
appear on pages 99–100, which constitute an extension of
the copyright page.

Library of Congress Cataloging-in-Publication Data
Names: Hogan, Laura Reece, 1966- author.
Title: Butterfly nebula / Laura Reece Hogan.
Description: Lincoln : The Backwaters Press, an imprint
of the University of Nebraska Press, [2023] | Series: The
Backwaters Prize in Poetry
Identifiers: LCCN 2023009936
ISBN 9781496236104 (paperback)
ISBN 9781496237842 (epub)
ISBN 9781496237859 (pdf)
Subjects: BISAC: POETRY / American /
General | LCGFT: Poetry.
Classification: LCC PS3608.O482565 B88 2023 |
DDC 811/.6—dc23/eng/20230306
LC record available at https://lccn.loc.gov/2023009936

Designed and set in Cormorant by Mikala R. Kolander.

for Lisa
and
for my Beloved

Live the questions now. Perhaps you will then gradually, without noticing it, live along some distant day into the answer.

—RAINER MARIA RILKE, *Letters to a Young Poet*

You shall be called by a new name,
pronounced by the mouth of the Lord.

—ISAIAH 62:2

CONTENTS

III. CRUX

IV. TELESCOPIUM

V. PHOENIX

BUTTERFLY NEBULA

I

HYDRA

You divided the sea by your strength;
You broke the heads of the sea serpents in the waters.

—PSALM 74:13

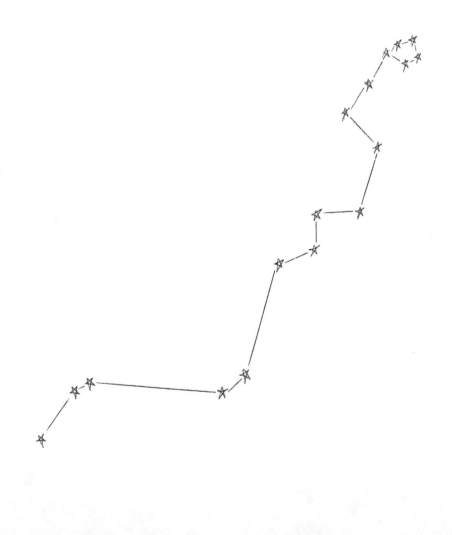

In Which I Pray for Stars

Remember me, Lord. Today I am half-buried
in the shallow sea floor off the coast of Guam.

The sunlight struts and strums the surface
but I am beneath, enclosed in this reticulated wreck,

I just don't know it, don't know anything
except this tight place, wearing your crown-of-thorns

sea star. I first met your ocean in the air, in the hull
of a military cargo aircraft not meant for little girls,

the tattered safety harness dangling useless
over my slight shoulders, the orange wax earplugs

given to me against the deafening engines too gigantic
for my ears. I was a container, I was shipped out

to a cold war zone. I plummeted the same way
I rocketed over waves, guided ballistics as an exercise.

The submarine's mark for target practice.
I could be diving for man-of-war jellyfish, I could be

sailing the moon, I could be flying to a tiny coral island
on a missile range. Yes, I could be doing that, I could still

be doing that. I rise before dawn and sing psalm-stars
into the ocean sky. You remembered Noah out

of floodwaters, the Israelites out of Egypt, Rachel into
conception of a protostar. I say this in hope.

I say this to jog your immense multiverse of memory,
slanted as the shaft of an arrow aching

for release. How we push at the water while it lifts
and sinks, turns and crashes at your word.

Your remembering is not really that,
Lord, it is supernova, and the fusion that makes new stars.

It is activation. Resurrection.
Dismembering on the one side and re-

assembly on the other. I am in the hull.

Longing as Dark Matter

The most rending   most revealing   most propelling
substance,   driving us   with sugared whip

of desire   and the astronomers say
this lack   makes up the vast majority   of matter

or matters   in the universe   and I think they must know
how to send instruments into space to track it

they must know   how to isolate   the absence
which pulsates   in bones aching   for what they need

or think they need   in the marrow   that sucks
everything out of orbit.   The astronomers know

how to extract   information   from astrophysical objects
make them spill the truth   detect proof

in the way the stars   sway in unison,   in the way
the universe   bows and bends aside   to allow for the ghost

of it to pass.
We can measure   the gravitational effects

on surrounding matter   on blood vessels   pupils
airways   pulse rates   tear ducts   we can observe it

slashing a hole right through—
astronomers stalk   their prey covetously   track the prints

of its wild   and ruthless ricocheting.
It has been searched for intensely   and never seized

only the telltale damage   left behind in the wakes
ripped in constellations,   the unseeable fault lines

in the soul   keening   the shrill want   to know
to touch   to have.   But so invisibly   it pierces

the fabric of being   with an arrow   that is phantasm
of fire   thrusting fire   into fire that already burns

slow   in the lamp   of every star.

Heart as Siphonophore

The researchers had imagined it, whipsawing
        through silty sleeves,

the giant siphonophore, sea worm of such ghostly
        fiber and length it would take hours

to watch it pass, the writhing blue bioluminescent
        skin of it simultaneously here and far.

Now they witness it, photograph it, stare
        at the improbable, slithering 150-foot

figment, ribboning in a quantum
        state, the floating bell of head so distant

from the end of its colonized chambers
        that the steadiness steers far from the fret—

stingers jostle in the eerie suck and ripple of its path.
        Now, *Praya dubia*, leap and swim forward

with sureness, now, wind sideways in uncertain fatigue.
        The head arrives in an Australian oceanic canyon,

while the tail trails in a different time zone. So far
        from true cadence of itself, two places at once:

there, the water glows aqua in your presence,
        and here, the long, thin muscle still heaving,

reaching along the night-drenched bottom.

Heart Nebula

Red hydrogen gas
and dust become the blood
glowing in contour of cardiac flesh,
turned on its side the universal symbol:
two lobes as one. What surges from the center
shapes the ruby shine, tenderness on streaming stellar
wind. The human heart, tiny cradle of light, holds at its
core these stars. The aching burn blows up the distance,
a reaching ardor in your chest. It will bloom out and
lead you into fervent spilling over into the galaxy,
expanding if you let it. Or you could cover
it with shade and fear, and leave it many
light-years far away, lost in the cold
compartment of space.

HR 6819 and the Lovesick Be Star

Be star, so in love he sheds his shine
    like a skin, spinning

300 miles per second, so woozy
    with all that extra fire

the desire arcs   levitates
    from the surface, emits

flares of longing even to earth.
    O Be star, swooning blue

frenzy, circling dear inner star, who
    circles a mysterious third object
    —an eternal triangle.

O inner star, dreaming of that tall dark
    bad boy, so powerfully absent,

so magnetic he commands her orbit, eats
    her sparkle, feeds on her verve.

O presumptive black hole, in fact
    supermassive

        black hole, drawing her

inexorably. O earthlings, who mistake
    star-crossed entanglement

        for light.

Eye as Firework Jellyfish

I am not crushed here in the darkness,
plunged sea-deep in you. I float
the midnight zone, soundless and invisible
but for your light, startling.

An eye woken this way flares alert,
knows now its flat existence before,
monochrome jelly wafting
through nothing—until you.

Then the blank aquatic dusk shimmers
incandescent. Then, reflective, the slit
blinks electric: fluorescent
rays ring the iris of cobalt.

The aperture of pupil opens, bulb
of cornea an eerie cast of blue—
the ghost refracted upside down
five thousand feet below the surface.

Lamp of my socket, you ignite
the submerged fuse, spark
starburst of sight, fathoms
below any disturbance of waves.

Psyche as Vampire Squid

She'd like them to believe she's dangerous
as a matter of self-preservation. She sharpens

each spike for the deep-sea cosplay, inverts
the collar of skeletal spines,

but it's all a big show for the predators. She tricks
her ink colorless, throws in a pinch

of bioluminescence in a classic defense response
to snatch eyes to twinkle lights

while she flees. But you. She'd like you to believe
she's harmless. She wants to see you, wants

to know who she loves there in the dark. She holds
a candle or glint of knife

at the end of every arm,
warm allure just for you. She is neither octopus

nor vampire but she thirsts for what's under
the skin. She'd like you to see

the Cupid you've become; she'd like
to sink into your soul.

The Dark Rift

To read in reverse, by contour and correspondence,
the cupped wingspan of partridge alighting

by the celestial river to drink
brightness from the Milky Way, blazing cascade

in contrast to the dusky edge which knifes
sideways through starlight. The Incas translated

the shadow spaces. The dark rift carves absence
and image: the thirst of bodies.

A llama mother and baby panting, tongue of fox,
toad splayed midleap, snake arrowing to sparkle

of all that pours dazzling and good. The silhouettes only,
but we know them, we name

our own longings in those empty places in the night sky,
parched mouths open wide in a pattern

that tells of hidden hollows. How we desire
to be known, even just in outline. How we ache to form

that precise imprint, dark nebula cradling new stars,
in the secret constellation of another's heart.

Oyster Nebula

You knew I'd trade away everything I have
for you. You knew I'd fall in love with your
radiance, tender and consuming. My fingers
drop the moon and sun
to reach for you, beyond space, and inscribed
here across fleshy grooves where the irritant
must lodge in the crease of nebular tongue,
gloss layered gossamer over each ripped veil.
Last night I dreamed
blood inside the body was blue, bluest sapphire,
rainiest indigo, that blood was only red when
struck and drawn from the body. Hidden blue
of my heart-vein, you sift your grain of sand
until I shift iridescent, until I break red and bead
into milky pink, rose. I tell you a mystery—
astronomers see the brightness of the nebula's pearl
as variable, conclude it is two stars though observing
only one pulse, a single glazed shine.

Sea Butterfly

Pallid smallness of ocean, sometimes called
sea snail, your whole life

you steer by calcification, let the shell-weight
drop you like a plumb line

into pelagic murk, rough calculus of safety.
Water columns and gravity your

pantomime of control. The tiny
pulsing of mollusk code spells,

repeats, spells: survive.
The sinking of your little sub over and over

becomes the familiar tide, anchor
to yourself. But now you stir to shift

frailty into sail. Now to unfurl
transparent shuddering wisp

into a stubborn rising against the brute
current. You unfold defiance

through the gash
in your armor, a reticulated mouth

open to the world. The tongue tender beating
lobes, announcing battle. What you swim

reverses the momentum. What you loft higher
names itself.

Question Mark Butterfly

On your upper side, an ardent fire
makes promises. On your underside

rots a tattoo of death. Ova, larva, pupa,
imago—now you are the image of us,

half-buried in your mottled grays
and browns of what has fallen

to the forest floor, matted and decaying
into a final nothingness, yet

here among the counterfeit dead
foliage you pose one small

question, a silver curve and dot,
intended to confuse, or cry

one mock dewdrop, a masquerade
against birds. Are you dead or alive?

Were you given life to wear death,
until death wears you down?

To honor the riddle of the glittering mark
that names you

on painted icon of corrosion, all while
the vivid surface of life burns on?

Trembling Aspen: Needle

When tall neighbors shadow the understory, when need for the shining is shaded under a far-flung roof of leaves, the aspen chooses smallness, the squat, humble door into the Bethlehem cathedral, the narrowing way. There will be no glorious ascent without the felling. There will be no touching sun without the lower branches dropping to ground. The trunk becomes the needle, offers its eye for dromedaries. The trampling to collapse, the slow constriction in the throat, stoppering of breath. The rich routes of silk, flow of fluids cut. What would you call this sawing off of self, branch by branch, leaving only the scars, the blackeye knobs scissoring up the bark, tracks of phantom limbs? The park service calls it self-pruning. The ranger calls it necessary shedding. The biologist calls it a sharp little trick of abscission. It's a stab of death for life, surgery to rise higher, reach sunshine. The sewing up of each mouth in order to speak sky.

Fireball

Name the physics of such a trajectory, of stone leaving
        the sling, of meteorite grazing the atmosphere

after midnight, green flashing ball with twist of tail
        skimming the Pilbara sky. A stone from the river,

or from interstellar space, a chosen rock taken up and flung
        with a finesse beyond. The astounded Australian

night owls gape at the green sparking spectacle. The rock
        strikes the millimeter of the giant's forehead, dead

accurate. We will never find them, these fireballs, once
        all that superheated air vaporizes and only the pebble

is left. We will never find the iron rock among iron rocks
        in the Pilbara outback, in the Vale of the Terebinth.

And yet the story. The pyrotechnic glow of your perfect
        path. How the slightest may be the shooting star. How

you propel us with aim and timing. We squint to observe
        the miracle: the flick of your wrist, the shining stone.

Your Never and Always Ring of Fire

Sometimes only a hand,   your hand,   comes between us
and death.   Moses, who begged to see,   you shielded from

your passing glory;   you loved too much to say no.   Can you
feel   our nearest passing by of you,   the bride languishing

for the light of you,   the sight of you,   setting in her nothing?
Sometimes you put the whole   far moon   between us

just to return her love   sometimes in a new moon invisible
she feels the blister   of your passion   a presence

hidden in the gloss   of absence.   Sometimes at apogee,
the farthest point   when earth, moon, and sun   you align

in lunar node   you shelter her   crown the daytime night sky
with a marriage   of fire and not   never and always;

dark disk steadily bites into bright   eclipses the eyes.
Except for the longing   there is no prayer for this.

Sometimes only a hand   your hand   holds the moon
just so   pours molten fire   into perfect annulus

one minute twenty second   slender, blazing   ring of promise
for your dearest love,   dearest passing shadow.

Via Negativa: New Moon

Why do I want the moon, which belongs
to you? Why do I drive against the foothills
like a maniac to moon hunt, when it's gone
missing? I don't understand
what's happening to my physics. I might
need to live in a tent for a month, away
from streetlights and other blazes. I
might need a blade, need to cut
my hair and nails to slimmest crescents
and solve for white-pleated wings of moth,
sprung whole from phases, just to die
for light. You've packed up the not-
moon tonight, a hanging
promise: your light will come.
Go barefoot in the drought-powdered dirt.
Press hard against the hull
of cocoon. The strongest sit in the dust,
unknowing. The strongest
linger in the bind, wait
for faintest sliver,
emerge.

II

MICROSCOPIUM

I am a ghost waiting to be made flesh by love
I am too imperfect to bear.
—ROBERT CORDING,
"Advent Stanzas"

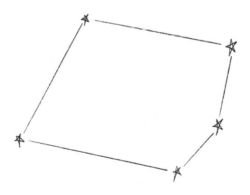

Butterfly Nebula

A stellar death must herald it—   the hottest star
        throws off its envelope. Torus of dust

eaten and retched   all its life.   Two violent jets
of gases over 36,000 degrees Fahrenheit   must rip

across space   many heavy light-years
        out from under

tightened belt of the body,   dark slit
running   through the waist.   A disk of weight, a thumb

of the divine pinches   the butterfly almost
to severing.   The thing about a resurrection—

        the chrysalis must cleave   expel the life blood
                damp crushed wings

at first unrecognizable. The Magdalene looked
        in all the wrong places. She

thought he was the gardener.   The split-apart vowels
of her name   uttered   unfold

across constellation,   stretching   stream
of ultraviolet radiation   making cast-off skin of the dead

star glow   in two arching nebular lobes   its new form
        still gathering energy.

Prayer for Traversing the Eye

If I molt
peel and cast
the assemblage,
push aside / bend
behind can I sliver
shiver atoms spectral
can you splinter me
cut down the camel
of me shatter me
until I shed me
can you shove
me through
this frail
slit?

The Elysia Sea Slug

I will give you a new heart and place a new spirit
within you, taking from your bodies your stony
hearts and giving you natural hearts.
—EZEKIEL 36:26

Things go sideways. The body opens the wrong
doors and lets in bad company, copepods that take over.
Then we carry it, segments crippled with parasites,

stony growth. I think you mean it when you say
you'll give me a new heart. I see evidence in stars,
in the sea slug that can detach its entire diseased body

and crawl away on orange horned antennae. The head
births a new form. Mangled sea stars
and flatworms do this, but only the Elysia sea slug

sprouts a heart from just a head. This is your prescription.
You pry loose the cargo and craft fresh strands of light.
When I unhook all the parts

and struggle away, won't you come rebuild? Tear down
the years the locusts have eaten, let the heavy consignment fall.
Regenerate a glistening wholeness from only one piece.

Let that piece be you.

Soul Nebula

You have grappled to open
the door, over

and over. You wonder
why the inside must be swept clear

so violently,
the aching cavities carved

by radiation and stellar winds streaming
from massive O stars

far too dazzling
to see. The destruction sweeps

the dark vacuum
with loneliness—yet, hollow

the nest. Empty the hidden spaces
of the glimmering nursery

within you,
forming pure new light. Baby suns

stud the rim
of waiting. Every possibility belongs

to the expansion that unlocks
the chamber, pushes wide

the portal,
sets the stars to ignite.

Leafy Sea Dragon

The olive-tinted appendages sway
in time with the kelp. As if they were

fronds, as if the fiercely fragile dragon
body were not. As if the dappled

branches were locomotive,
and transparent fins were not. As if

the camouflaged pipette of snout
preferred the element of fire.

As if Daphne paused, her tendrils
sprouting, her feet budding seagrass

rootedness. As if fearless, never
dabbling in greens and barks

to match the tangle of seaweed. As if
conqueror, wreathed in sea-blessed laurels,

astride the current. As if hiddenness
marshals victory.

Playing with Tiger Sharks
on the Missile Range

We were shrewd on an adventure, like Huck Finn.
She was six, I was eight. We set out to hike
the entire boomerang of the island. We took
peanut butter sandwiches in a purple bandana,
flip-flopped to the rocks

at ocean's edge. My sister and I knew
our matching denim with stars had superpowers,
like Wonder Woman, so we climbed, our spindly
legs slipping. We knew the glistening indigo spikes

of the sea urchin, the orange and blue-splotched coral,
the dark manta shadow, knew the sea
held shell-encrusted *Treasure Island* chests of gold.
How thrilled we were to spot the shiny fin

of a little tiger shark, a friend
like Baloo, Bagheera, the striped body undulating
in the clear Micronesian water, so close
we could almost touch it, then another. Another.

We were captivated that they followed us,
impressed by our daring plan, wanting to play.
If we'd seen a flash of light, say, over nearby Bikini,
an immense boiling mushroom over the sea,
we would have looked for Alice's caterpillar.

Manatee Nebula

Grow ever tender lolling on the razor rocks, belly out.
Slow, curious, trusting. Graze the pickerel weed, water
hyacinth, turtle grass. The sea my blustery bed, sky
my blue forgiving. Mistaken for mermaid, misheard.
Fed a twisting tune, wrong song at the surface. Mis-
herded, propeller whipped. Grow hide over hurt. Scab
over ship strikes. Scar over spiral-cut scar. Meander silky,
like I own the star fields, trailing my own shredded
skin. Always the vulnerable swathes, mammaries, whiskers,
slashed tail. The venerable slacken it, know how to slide
softness into sea. They know themselves: elastic
and ephemeral. It is still alive, what you left in me,
glinting with scars, gliding to mangrove leaves, to nova.

Crab Nebula

Franco Pacini parsed the delicate filaments,
contemplating the puzzle box of brightness, pressing

intricate panels into prediction. Eight years later
the neutron star slid and snapped into sight,

but like many pulsars, its speech
scattered into brittle rays that stammer.

The tenacity of astronomers, mulish beachcombers
calmly waving metal detectors day in and day out.

Sifting grains of sand, collecting each discarded exoskeleton
studding the shore as evidence. They pass their buckets

and bravado on to the next, and the next, for the work is long.
The pulsar wind of the nebula streams, stirs the heart,

and while that convoluted flesh still beats, it will intractably
scramble sideways,

reach with swagger. Fiddler crabs, once wounded, are known
for dishonest signaling.

They wave the regrown major claw with the energy
of a supernova, while all along they know

its true weakness, the shattering secreted in brandished light.

Lyrebird

This poem wanted to rhapsodize
about the love song of the superb

lyrebird (his real name), who flares
tail and struts atop his display area, a stage

that he erects for his desired mate.
He mimics every bird (a few) of every species

(not even close) in fantastic vocalization
never before heard (true) in all of Australia

or the world—a mobbing throng of songbirds,
fricative squawks and trilling cries of panic

at the approach of a predator (frantic
wingbeats included). This poem ached

to swoon at the skill and ardor
laid at her passerine feet. But the liar

bird, it turns out, sings to deceive her
into thinking she cannot leave him because

she will be attacked instantly by a predator
(as she is), and as he mounts her, he covers

her eyes with a hood of his beating wings.

Letter

I will stand at my guard post . . .
keep watch to see what he will say to me.
—HABAKKUK 2:1

The upright scrawl of leaf
cleaving last to the fig tree I mistake

each daybreak for the bird-messenger,
the one that I am sure will come

flare the mouth of morning. The Psalmist
says you are faithful, you are just;

give answer. Not in predawn darkness
which dims my discerning, not in crashing

confusion from the street, please,
but in yellow murmur of petals, dropping

cursive of honey, low liminal hum
of bees. You are tender, you are gentle; give

syllables of yourself in spilling light. Wings
of white-throated swift, the slow opening

of pinecone, release of seed, snowcap roses
in loosening splendor. My written hand—

clay and so near ground, held up
to you, empty—waits

if not quite for an answer, then for some sprig
or scribble from you.

Soul as Half Moon

Let me just glimpse
the undiscovered terrain in phases, my hidden

mouth half-open with prayer of lustrous sun.
We are not lesser lights.

The illuminated half holds the mystery of itself
in crescent arms. Faint earthshine bathes

what I can barely discern as a wholeness
against the black void

of space. You and I stare to pin down
the ghost half,

materializing then vanishing. It may take
a whole life to know that the dark of the moon

differs from the night,
that what is bright and what is baffling

orb together, full.

Universal Law of Turbulence

The mathematicians count on the report
of numbers to explain upheaval.

Take turbulence, a seeming chaos,
they divide neatly

into whirlpools of uncertainty, each to
its own. Then they solve turmoil

as a system, blue paint dropped
and twirled into red, stripes thick

and thinning, narrowing
thinnest into
purple.

They prove: a collapsing
ratio in the coming together

and splitting
apart, in swirls of river

whitewater, in tumbling of clouds
of cream poured into coffee—so too

in systems of love and grief: each
tapers
        into a single strand

just outside itself, then
swallows,

blurs.

On Finding the Atom Is Divisible

Pierre, when I write your name, it isn't letters,
but the word, whole and luminous, fused
to the center of me. I cannot explain your existence,
or the strong force pulling you into my life—you
who corresponded with me, fit every place in me
the others thought bizarre or masculine,
or too womanly to be brilliant. You saw me,
love. You met me at the core, electrons not stolen
but covalent, our bond so close you were my hands
and feet, link and freedom, the whirl
of brain into being. Our children—polonium,
radium. Irène and Ève. Nobel. The institutes,
the students, the long line of research after us.
Cancer therapies.

                        Atomic bombs.
No, we never spoke of the paradox: the heart
of our union, our discovery, was division. But just
like that it took over, dragged you under heavy
rain, crushing wheels of a horse-drawn carriage
on Rue Dauphine, split   me apart.
Even before, our worried glances, coughing,
the slow fissure of illness, of poisoning.
The chain reaction of my breaking, parting me further
from the Marie you cherished. But Pierre—I can't
account for discontinuities in each model, the way
you cross the uncrossable, charge me, you un-
fracture me even now in incomprehensible oneness,
still glowing, beyond my science.

Petri Dish

The researchers couldn't do without it,
so fungible, holder of the things
they want to observe, things they need to contain.
Originally made of glass, then polystyrene,
next given injection-molded ribs for stiffness—
handy strongbox for the unruly and weird.
One of them takes pipette and lab tweezers to the dish,
deposits the seed of a body part. She will cultivate this
like her Martha Washington geraniums.
On the inner flat of the dish, disembodied human
tear glands grow. The dish confines,
efficiently clasps without limbs.
The other researcher has hit on the cocktail
of neurotransmitters to make them cry. She drips
it into the dish over many days and the tear glands
swell with uncried tears. The ribs of the dish are silent,
unmoved; the dish lacks tear ducts,
so the tears build furiously inside the organoids,
they balloon almost to bursting—the dish blocks
them firmly, its borders unbreachable.

The Most Tiny Quantity of
Reality Ever Imagined

It's nothing, almost nothing,
it is the most tiny quantity of reality
ever imagined by a human being.
—FREDERICK REINES,
on detecting the neutrino

Just when we can mouth neutrino
you give us   muon neutrino.

Just when   we can swallow
this liquid alphabet

then tau neutrino   which nipples
the tongue   but you know

just how we will digest
the droplet,   integrate the particle.

Then you feed us milk we cannot name,
new nothing   in cosmic showers

blurting up   from the ice in Antarctica
in secret code   wanting to play.

When we reach   too far
you enfold us   in darkness,

hush and rock,   your lullaby
is time. *Time, you say, has not come.*

When you are bigger.

Moon Rust

It's very puzzling . . .
The moon is a terrible environment
for hematite to form in.
—SHUAI LI

Your profusion of rose on the moon
astonishes us, we who don't believe
in hopeless odds and frittered outcomes.

The ruddy flecks impossible in the limited
lunge of our science and brains, and mother
how you must smile

to watch us, baffled by our own tarnished
constrictions. We think we know
blemish, and sometimes we do,

but how difficult for us to see your hidden
hand switching for pristine, the way you take
the rusted-out bottom and make it sail straight.

You show your little ones the terse blanket
of moon's face, whisk it away to teach object
metamorphosis. You speak rush of red

into pale dead body. You gather the decayed
spokes and rims, corroded hinges, you know
our dust and blood better than we do.

With sleight of hand you write
on the moon in the ink we most despise,
that nothing is improbable for you, that

the blossom is never quite what we think.

III

CRUX

We have to be braver than we think we can be, because
God is constantly calling us to be more than we are.
—MADELEINE L'ENGLE, *Walking on Water*

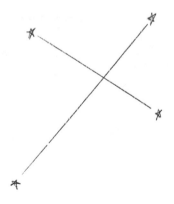

Coalsack Nebula

The mystics say to dig, hammer the cloud, day
and night. That the act of gazing at the long obsidian

robe of God undresses unknowing. I have descended
one mile underground down a mine shaft

in the back of a pickup and there was no adjusting
of the eyes, only the coal oblivion of open veins. I

have tracked the dark nebula at the foot of the Crux
600 light-years from earth and I cannot penetrate

your meaning, swathed in the opaque interstellar cloud
which erases young blue shine and sweeps light away

in dust of loss and blackness of grief. I cannot pierce
the absence to find a single ray. I am always imploring

you to tell me, beloved, if you have left me forever?
I scrabble the seam of your silence. You blot the belly

of earth, hollow the cosmos; you ink the endless empty
patches, you sharpen my unseeing eyes so I slip

the stars. You hew vast space for yourself in my narrow
atoms. I dimly carry this sparking quarry which slides

through my sieved soul. I am always asking you to untie
your sack of stars, all while here there are diamonds.

The Blue Hour

For Seung-Un

The duration depends on the latitude
    and the season, but the colder,

the longer the sheet of sky freezes
    gunboat blue, casts cerulean spell

over artic snow, icy ocean, cliff,
    and woman. New to bitter hue

of snow over ice over sea, she falls
    through the indigo. No one hears,

no one sees. It's a story she rehearses
    at night, the treading of water,

the keeping on, until she slowly stiffens
    in the coldest hour, that phase

of twilight when the sun is so far
    below the horizon the light

comes in clutched blue waves, when
    broken promises

drown the landscape. Nothing exists
    outside the mottling of blue

until the earth unpins the twilight. This
    is when I plead, earth—
                please turn.

Bow in the Clouds

In this global flood, could we
rely on a physics

beyond steep or flattened curves.
Perhaps we cannot summon

sudden vaccines, enough ventilators,
deduce how to stall, to bottle

the malevolent genie, to still
writhing horses of panic or slice

snaking lines around markets.
Yet consider the physics of light,

of sun and cloud, how the shine persists
out of sight. How the torrent

may become the prism. How Noah
kept sending the dove.

A Small Good Friday Service
at Notre Dame Cathedral

The blackened wound still festers, open to Paris sky,
barbs of melted steel beams left to untangle, all progress

stopped by pandemic. The irreplaceable roof and spire
lost; yet priceless treasure survived—the crown

of thorns, long-suffering. The nave billows toxic lead
from the incinerated roof. The structure teeters

on failure, construction helmets required.
Priests process in masks, liturgical actors read in plastic

suits, rubber boots, cameramen capture the scene
in hazard gear. Only of a few of us can be there, a few

of us playing all of us, all of us who wear hard hats
in adoration of a crown of thorns.

Holy Saturday

Lord, you know every alleyway and porch of my heart, the dirt paths, secret passages. You know, Lord of the land, the furrows of map, how the center of gravity holds, low and steady. You rush breeze through the trees, the scent of orange blossoms and jasmine fans day and night through the screen door. You unfold the floor plan, descend the cellar stairs, siphon the ache for water underground. In some sleight of hand you hull the missing, make visible the latent. How endlessly you translate the living—your unseen footsteps through sea, the mighty split. Root digging into the table of maggots. The throb of raven wings remaking your word, the double iris verging on purple kiss. The wild sunflower by the side of gravel road, sprung up overnight tall as a mailbox. The seed has broken open again. Will you free me, I ask, as you gently peel open the shades, pry the deadbolt, coax smallest tuft of green.

St. Teresa's Pillow

splintered block of wood   grooved, now behind glass
    in the Avila monastery   what dreams

if she could sleep   did she lie supine   or turn to press
    her skull, ear painful   to listen

for what's rigid, immobile   I am thinking of the slender neck
    ossifying at that angle   sometimes it hurts

too much to move ourselves   God tossed her
    like a ragdoll from a horse into seven inches of muck

if this is how you treat your friends   (she could get sassy
    with her love)   *then no wonder you have so few*

but he knows what he's about   knows
        when to throw us hard

when to carve away the comfort of ruts   bolt us   jolt
    us like Jacob   to wrangle

the dark dazzling weight of an angel   your unbearable
    finger   thrusts

unhinges my contending hip   (what did you think
    this rising   from the mud would look like?)

of the stone pillow   we make an altar   pour oil
    if we dream, painful   hear the new name

Mary, Wife of Clopas

My shape always shrouded in the possessive,
the other name so profuse
it fails as an identifier. Even so I am noteworthy
for being utterly unknown, men
have assigned me this grave or that—
mother of James and Joseph, wife of Joseph's
brother, or daughter of Clopas, or another
Mary altogether, the word crassly welded,
wielded wrong. But they all nod, agree
I was there at the foot
of the hideous that day, that my bones shook,
wracked with wailing, that your mother and I
gripped each other until nail marks
purpled our arms. That I led her home howling,
eyes swollen shut. That the morning
after the sabbath, silent in transfixed grief
we stumbled with our aloes, spices, linen
to the rock-hewn hole and found you
not gone. When all of them thought
you were a ghost, I knew
you were more real than any of us. I who am not,
a ghost. Your words crossed the ether
and I saw my outline. Not that my being,
belonging to all except me, became yours;
but that you cradled my calloused hands
weighed with the jar of myrrh, looked
me in the eyes. You unearthed what was dead
and it sat up, breathing.

Ghost Nebula

Touch me and see, because a ghost does not
have flesh and bones as you can see I have.
—LUKE 24:39

So easily startled by vastness, dark
distances, arrival, they were terrified by him
that night glimmering in their midst.
Jesus knew they needed to finger the familiar
relief of bones under warm flesh to believe
the body, pale star
studding their peripheral vision, a specter
rattling even Peter, who had seen the not-
ghost of him before, walking the sea. Jesus
knew their need to know he hungered, tasted
the tilapia baked in olive oil with salt, lemon,
tangy fingers to mouth.

                We also mistake for shade
his spilling, think we grasp the ghost of him
across the universe—filaments of light,
nebular veils. His words cast the contours,
recognizable until we see the not-
dead of him, our terrified minds
opened to enormity, but gently. How he fishes,
the rock and creak of boat, rough coils of net,
convinces us to touch
the wooden hull, that we know this rising
scent of salt on interstellar wind, drifting shape
of wave, of star, simple as flesh and blood.

On Neptune It Rains Diamonds

What gems crystallize
beneath that distant blue surface? I

could only gaze the lens,
guess at secrets   make hypotheses

about what was happening
between the layers. On Neptune,

below a hydrogen-helium atmosphere lies

ice   compressed and flamed to melting—

    I wonder at this oscillation
       of force and

fire—

the carbon and methane chemically react,
and no reversal: billions

of diamonds   fall in a glitter,
bond, encase the core. How

could I know until the rain perforated
   that day,   what can I do

except shine, wonder at the trove
of a planet so far from me as to appear

nearest,   whether that is
a trick of telescope.

Geminids

Past November, past midnight,
you pull and release

whole quivers of whizzing silver shafts
into the indigo night. If I could dilate

wide enough, I'd catch
each shooting signal, let through each spark

of sight. Your words throw open
my tight shutters, spangle the black mountains,

enkindle falling diamonds,
cherished as folktales: a new baby's soul

descending, an angel in flight, the rhythmic flare
of wish and wish again—

that it might be so. That we still have time.
That you mean to give love. That pure starlight

streams the horizon. That constellations leap
across the atmosphere in a blazing embrace.

To see a waltz of Geminids, magic in the sky.
The reality is: they are tiny grains of space dust.

The reality is: so am I.
We skim across the surface of the world, dust

to dust, brief powders of fire, sure short arrows.
The reality is: eternally

we are incandescent casements
of your celestial light.

Ribbons

St. Thérèse of Lisieux, asked as a child
to select a ribbon: *I choose all.*

You know what it's like
to want it all: velvet, taffeta, lace,

butter-yellow, hazel, sky,
the basketful. You know how

to expect a heaven where a little flower
gets every meadow of love. You know

what it costs to take them up, one
by one, the ribbons you desire,

black-striped and gossamer, to take
the darkness and the light of him,

to wear them with equal joy,
marks of love

and love's repayment.
You know the way to hold out

prayerful hands, gathering the cries
of your daisy-chain children,

clutching them in bright handfuls,
choosing.

Super Supernova

The hawk doubled back
to confront the orbiting raven

that had attacked its counterpart.
It was the two of them

that made this match possible.
The two massive stars merged

before exploding,
the brightest supernova ever recorded,

five times the observable
light of the usual lonely supernova.

Binary stellar collision, called
super supernova, called

           third heaven.
Come, take my devotion,

I am but burn of mirrored ray.
Latch it to the shimmer

of twinned solitude,
let the gravitational pull

exert force. Give me your star-flare
words, your radiant exponential.

Lean, fire,
           into the collapsing kiss.

Trembling Aspen: Twine

They can't help themselves, they clasp hands underground, they point to heaven and quake. They instinctively make a whole forest of themselves. A cathedral sewn into existence by a force beyond them. How the columns of white smooth bark brace the vaulted roof, lime green then living gold. Invisible walls breathe crisp mountain air. The mulch of discarded leaves and insect bodies patterns the rich floor, not ground but ceiling, sprouting seam above infinite iterations of this life together. The oldest living organism is not leviathan, or sequoia, but the aspen in Utah's Fishlake Forest. Eighty thousand years old, the roots twine in one long embrace, thread and knot through earth, through centuries, the constant story unfolding in my heart, in your heart, in the interlocked heartbeat of every tender sapling breaking the surface,

Exchange

When he arrives hooded in words,
he offers vowels of white vestments
that I recognize. I take them
on my tongue, savor my true dialect.
I give him the chrysalis of myself.

When he arrives with beam of lantern,
he unrolls parchments which spark
stars of bells and time. I feast
on his feast. I can only give him
the empty nest of this hunger.

But he eats it. When he comes
he pulls a pigeon from my breast,
unfurls the scarlet longing for heaven.
I can only give him the burning sky,
which I find slipped into my pocket.

When he returns from his journey,
he gives me light to remember him by,
instructs me to squint and enter
sideways. Blind as moon, I climb
the spiraling hawks. When he comes

quietly with his lapis, he paints a sea
that catches my breath.
When he waits at the window,
when he waits at his just-open window,

I pray murmurations of starlings; that one
might swoop through the slender silence
he has left ajar
for me.

Cocoon

> And you will see how we see God,
> as well as ourselves placed inside His greatness,
> as this little silkworm within its cocoon.
> —TERESA OF AVILA

At the center of the winter-dark room,
The Cloud of Unknowing smolders and we read
ourselves. We take turns, you and I, rapt
with anonymous warnings, promised disclosure.

Sometimes you vanish into your bank of cloud
and leave no stars. I can only wait.
But you always come back with more to tell me.
The place is rife with risk—words rising up

through the raw. Is this your keyboard or mine?
It's grown wild with green turning tendrils,
honeysuckle, milkweed. So much changing,
so much I can't seem to figure out,

but the knitting warmth surges along
the emerald seams and we write it out in long lines
that won't stir to life. No—look at us, shifting.
At the center of the room shines

The Living Flame of Love, the ardent spark
enlivens, zags in electric arcs though the cloud,
your fire or mine, now it doesn't matter, we tend
this tenderness spilling across the distal floorboards,

blazing, the slant of ceiling, floor falling away,
the wing unripe and unasked-for now come to term,
a tongue thrusting through quick recitation,
through the words you want us to inhabit. This habit

we have grown of one speech. Here is what you say
in the burning under the words you write
in me (I write these words you write in me)—
be this alchemy. Break through, beloved.

Our time twining this way has done something.

IV

TELESCOPIUM

Although the resurrection *of* the body is
future, resurrection *in* the body is present.
—MICHAEL J. GORMAN, *Participating in Christ*

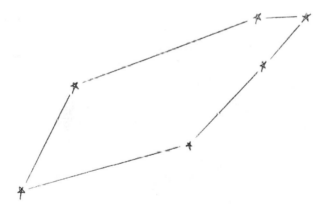

Petition as Praying Mantis

Maybe I should question my questions. Maybe
    I should breathe in the unruly garden, covet

the electric green fulcrum and bulging eyes of the praying
    mantis, motionless. The taut focus on the cricket,

leafhopper, lizard, the sloping stalk and spring. The lime
    peel camouflage. The way it preys barefoot.

A steep posture of single-minded hunger
    that consumes. Nothing can starve it out. Are we not

our most ardent desire? It carves us hip to heel, sculpts
    spine. We are witnessed this way. Reeled backward,

an indrawn tongue with mosquito. The praying mantis
    is known to devour small birds, to crave hummingbirds.

You open your hand and float me with ruby-throated
    iridescence, candlepower. In the magical blur and whir

I hover and sip   while you sing me,
    un-need me of answer.

Morpho Butterfly

At first in stillness I saw brown muted gray,
ventral bronze eyespots stared. As I stirred

a different color came to me—not one of earth
but of light, playing

across the dorsal surface of wings in waves,
teasing the nanoscale, perfectly parallel

veins of chitin and air spilling blue into eyes,
a dazzle of intensified light: crest

meeting crest in phase. Yet also diffraction
of crest which crosses

trough. The hand of Morpheus also gathers
what is out of phase,

startles the sleeper awake
to the vivid. I blink open to wings flickering

away, sapphire dashes on a map, the work
of metamorphosis steering.

Gedankenexperiment

Let us take two charged particles, call them
you and me. Let us set them far apart.

In theory, electromagnetic waves influence
each other to the end of the universe, whatever

has happened to the source. When I hike
through the hills and you call, the connection

drops. In the silence, spread alabaster wings
of a hawk recline on taut breeze in the canyon,

the shouldering movement delayed
just slightly in response to the gentle unfurling

force, the way your call comes through
later, how the conversation bends and turns,

takes time, the way your words ride wavelengths,
carry energy, then vanish into air.

Fear as Absent Mountain Lion

At the trailhead, a hand-lettered cardboard sign:
large mountain lion sighted. Here, yesterday

at this time—be alert. This is my trail,
back of my hand, but my eyes race up the foothills,

comb grasses and scrub. Odds of feline caution
or boldness shift and shadow. My own soft

deliciousness, weighed. I walk in a landscape of un-
anticipated pounce and claw, risk

crouching on the ridge. Here, the teeth of every stopping—
　　　　—countered by the steady pant

of every perseverance, purple fix on the wild
lavender and sage, yellow skim of finch

and cottontail through chaparral, crunch
of free terrain. My slow loping muscle,

gamboling sinew,
　　　　　　　　hunger set loose across the dust.

Hope as Alpha Centauri AB

Hope is not a hypothetical star.
                                        It is a luminous duo

    orbiting next door,
its ceaseless bright sway of photons always arriving

at the speed of light,
                                        flickering
    through the fractures.

Hope is not the brainchild of a genius, a theory
to span the gaps

between known
    and unknown facts, not a frozen star to
sputter

a dim prospect, a blitzar to battle doomed collapse
    through harrowing gates
      of a black
        hole,

or an imagined
    quark star springing eternal and strange.

    No,
it is our nearest star, a fiery reality speaking to each dark
    tripwire that ruptures
      your heart.

It is the candle
on the sidewalk, the nurse not giving up, the teacher making

space for the pressures of the room, the tensing future held
in the present.

Hope is the binary star, the solidarity
that appears as one sure shine.

It winks, precedes.
It never fails to traverse the night.

The Mother Gives Us

the sky and flaxen goldenrod in sheaves
tied in fragrant bundles to remind us
of earth from which we came. The mother
tells us this whole year sings in the cattails,
the woody rushes by the pond
hidden off dry gulch road, where larks
stitch their nests. She gathers the stems
of song in her mantle, draws up soft signaling
grasses of low mountain valley, tucks us in
with little hinged grasshoppers and purple butterflies.
She takes up the weaving of lullaby,
in gentle croon of creek and insect wing.
We feel it swathe us, wisp and feather
of sky, wild rumpling tones of hawk and owl
gathered in close, the good thread of story she hums,
spirals of daring flight, the moon crossing slow to silver
fullness, spilling milk all over the field.

Ophelia in Los Angeles

She would think better of it. She would shed
the capsizing layers of skirt. She would wedge-cut

the tresses, say good riddance to tangle.
She would get herself to an ice creamery. Or brewery.

She would know every nursery and flower shop
on the boulevard, choose roses over rue, plant

giant chrysanthemums in the yard. She would rock out
to her own breakup song. She would own

a good wetsuit. She would tell him about the other fish
in the sea, then dive the waves and glide.

Comet NEOWISE, July 4th

Are you coming
or going, radiant
sight? Rocketing to say—
now! I have come,
into my own, at last! Or,
tailed light,
to mark the exit
I have awaited
since you were born?
On the day of nearest passing
by the sun, dangerous
perihelion, maybe you also
were afraid
the nucleus would blister, yet
you traveled intact,
shooting behind the divine
advance, trailing a fan
of shimmering yellow
stardust. I rise early
to find you
above the horizon, my binoculars
trace your path, follow
the parabolic arc
blown by solar wind,
unfolding into the celestial beauty
of this arrival,
this passage, my firework
flung free.

Iris Nebula

You burst bulb, shoot stalk, shift the blue
spectrum in me. You take me to yourself
as light weds water, shimmers
for a thousand years in oceans translucent.

What is it about your fiery unsayable? It draws me
speechless into twilight, purple petals
open

—only you shiver cellulose and star—

open
on horizon, where words stunt and wilt.
The shine unseams me.

You murmur the lavender depths, remake
the reflection. What is it about the cobalt sway, your
unlost

liquid letters? You slowly mouth the syllables
of my secret name,
here and light-years away. You unbend,
suffuse each bloom of blue.

Comma Butterfly

A prophet folded may appear to be dead
leaf, but that prayer hides the burning

of the upper wings, the exoskeleton a prison
of consuming fire. A prophet feeds

on your word, bears your name in the form
of slivered comma—she is punctuation

bracketing the flame of your speech. She
emerges when yet again the barbs

of your beloved children stab along
your tongue. She glows orange with the effort

of articulating you, antennae rapt, vibrant
body alight among the decomposing

leaves strewn across the yard. She is hooded
in life, wears the spindly carbon mantle

of death, can only trust the chiseled curve
on each wing, tiny mirages

of oasis, half-moon watering holes
for the thirsty. She declares the grammar

of hope, parses your righteousness
over millennia. These daughters must stream

through pages of sky, your ardent rejoinders
in a series of ragged breaths.

Sign of the Times

You warned of this. The acid rain falling
        beyond our awareness—we've grown

                so dull after all these years
                        I barely

perceive the fig, hanging lower, ready
        to part, at last, from the tree. An accrual

                of sweetness, wrought by you—
                        see

how we are in it now: this ripeness   requires
        reaping.

                The enormous morning star beckons

        follow to the snug cabin, to
                the fire lit

safe from winter's frigid cloud of breath, deep snow.
        What makes me believe my snow blindness

                cured and cast behind me? Only you—
                        but please

be the answer to my question. Open my eyes
        to the widening hips of wisdom, the fruit's

                radiating complexion—

let stem and fig prophesy
        that time has come. We glimpse now

                your nearness.

Terror Weather

Now we predict house fires.
A horoscope of straw, a thousand lightning strikes.
This was supposed to be a conversation, but you are listening
to a podcast about longevity. I think about the longevity
of matchsticks, of chaparral. A red flag warning is deemed
too unalarming, so an extreme red flag is issued. Inevitability
scrapes, catches. When fire erupts in the 5 percent humidity
you view it casually, as from across a rain forest
or nearby planet. This ought to be a dialogue, but I rush
to gather photos and bronzed baby shoes, letters and journals
while you flip the news channels. The flames explode
across the valley while you check official social media accounts
and my snatches of speech hurry up and down the stairs alone.
We differ on the meaning of warning, of exponential rise
in temperatures, of mandatory evacuation. A top priority talk
should have happened but gusts of 70 miles per hour
blast embers into atmosphere, under eaves, the palm detonates
like a Roman candle, and being on two different pages
no longer matters because the book, all the books,
and the house are burning.

Approaching the Event Horizon

Under the crepe myrtle the sturdy earth seems
    fixed—who knows whether physicists
  waste their time trying to figure out time,

    or whether things shift
beyond our gray matter. Who can say if monks
  parse the hours wisely with prayer, climbing

invisible trees of transmutation. They reach
    limbs only to discern how the branches go on
  varying endlessly in vast mirror

    multiverse roots in the undug dirt. Black holes
behave sometimes as night, sometimes light-
    drenched passages for darting particles

or angels. Who knows whether you or I could step
  or fly through the door, somehow unshredded,
    someway bright, unpulverized, see the math

of God. The myrtle pushes roots down beneath
    me, and I curl quiet, breathing, yet to emerge,
woven in this whirling sphere. Even in shade

the light does its work, and like worm, root, frog,
    planet, nebula   singularity   I
  am one thing in the act of becoming another.

Resilience as Daffodil

Not aloe or jade, or elephant bush,
the thick skin of succulent. Not yucca,
or enduring cactus, stoic digging root
into rocky crag. The resilience I love

inhabits neither winter nor spring,
but grows in the curt ground prevailing
between: the tender shoot that spears
callous earth though barely dressed

in soft greenness. The contradiction
of gentle leaves unsheathing. No spike,
no thorn, merely the battery of bulb
buried deep, tiny suns startling the snow.

Between 50 and 51

The walls mimic grasscloth, an imagined savannah
of cream and palest green echoed in subtle stalks
on carpet. The beveled mirror on back wall, the panel
usual, buttons 1 to 60, but then that's all what my mind
reconstructs alone in the dark, in the panic and jangling
heart rate when the lights go out and the box rattles
and bangs against the shaking sides of shaft, dangling
on cords, on threads, dry metallic taste dumbing
my tongue. The distance matters, between you and me.
Between me and the ground, between terrifying plunges.
The weight of the car crashes, cracks. The cacophony
of shocked concrete heaves in my ears, screeches
in my bones. My hands flail, grapple
for anything. I should be on 51, walking to my beige office.
The drumming deafens now, no doors in the dead darkness
and my brain is frozen between the useless emergency
call button and the kind of prayer that is of the whole body,
of clamor and catastrophe, of take me and make me, of chaos
and clarity. My feet try to root into the pretend grasses,
but I lurch and sway with the casket or chrysalis.

Via Negativa: Corpse Flower

I have it backward, this stink of decomposition, this breaking
    apart of the body, lifeblood seeping into ground.

I've kept this for you, though I can't see what it is, buried
    this way. At the Huntington the gardeners cut

square windows with X-Acto knives into the expired calyx
    so we can view what trickery lies beneath the bruising

surface of the senses. The blossom is unpredictable, emerges
    from an underground corm just when you'd think

it's impossible. The fringe of petal, the color of dried blood,
    surrounds the spadix, a pale obelisk pointing skyward

in misdirection. When it matures you will want to run as far
    as your life will take you. You will want to be

anywhere but here, breathing the stench of rotting flesh.
    But here we are, wailing at the tomb while an angel

tries to open our minds to what is happening I can't inhale
    what's rising from the secret work of carrion beetles

and flies. I can't know your pollination, can only endure
    your dismantling hand, your new bloom not of my making.

V

PHOENIX

Who is this coming up from the desert,
leaning upon her lover?
—SONG OF SONGS 8:5

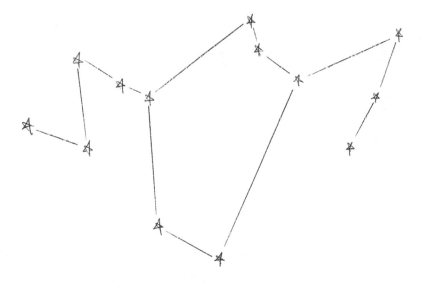

Fast Radio Bursts Detected
Close to Earth

Some tongues go undiscovered. Neutron stars,
for example, declare their own discourse. Radio
antennae prick with their fast untranslatable bursts.
Astronomers scrutinize the chat, Rosetta stone
splinters. They're so sure what they hear is story, but love,
I am fluent in the slivers under story. Of all the languages
you and *I* exchange, the most inaudible
feeds the need at its origin, the one that happened
at the dawning, at the original searing
wound. The compression that shaped your life, cut

you away from yourself. The vowels beyond vespers,
low and longing, are freedom. The consonants spill
space, vastness spelling over. You know this.
You will take up the slow expanse, tacit greening, wrap
yourself in swells of soft blue skyline
which you and *I* transmit in silent letters speeding
close to earth. You will soundlessly hum along to the hook
of my quiet chorus. You will know that *I* voice
and restore the light-years, that this box of hush is loud
with what only you receive.

We Are All God's Poems

When the word came down
that the illiterate should read the molten poems

of creation and re-creation, the artisans cast glass
line by lead line, in utterance of cathedral

body. Azure robe of Mary, weeping,
stripped skin of Francis, green of good

Samaritan, bending. Doorways
to heavenly Jerusalem, vivid verse enjambed

in jewel, letters for us, the living
poems spelling ourselves in water, metallic salt,

translucence and stain—not too short or long,
empty in middle space, flat, or falling down

to the crypt, but held in the possessive,
refracting sapphire, ruby, emerald, vibrant orange,

letting it all shine through. Each gaze lifted
intently, open palms catching soft shafts,

a text of becoming,
only fully realized in light.

Lazarus Rising

> Cataclysmic variables are binary systems. . . . The companion
> star loses material onto the white dwarf by accretion.
>
> —NASA

My corpse   a stellar core drained
of purpose   white dwarf assigned

to a frozen grave   and the sisters
weep. You spiral in

for the embrace,   companion
star, do the unthinkable   cast off

your own skin   to cloak the brother,
propel   life into the dead body

wrap me   in thick woolly winding
disk of accretion,   a transfusion

of mass   of you,   the point
of it leaving you   and entering

me   the source   the summit
the blurred line.   How could this end

if not in unbinding? You call me out   I stagger
into light   your spark   my breath—

this borrowing   made permanent.

Phoenix at Padre Serra Church

> During this vision a marvelously strange thing
> followed, for, as he himself afterward reported, the
> whole world, gathered together, as it were, under
> one beam of the sun, was presented before his eyes.
> —ST. GREGORY THE GREAT,
> describing the vision of St. Benedict

It is said all flesh is grass, flowers
which wither and fade away, that we are ashes
and to ashes we return

and I was walking slowly that day
through the church parking lot, the way you do
when going to a funeral, the way

you think about the dear one lost, try not
to focus on the metallic gray hearse,
rear doors flung open, look away

to see an out-of-season monarch butterfly,
the orange verging on crimson, a sun unfolding
the way the whole world

crimped in that single sunray collected in the eye
of St. Benedict, the physical world packed up
and then unpacked, photons redshifted

the way all this is a surface bursting
with tumbling ruby feathers of the maple, trailing
scarlet tail of roses blooming across

the rusted-out wrought iron fence, a collapsing

under the rising of something magnificent,
fire-plumed, gold-taloned,

brushing earth as if to scatter smallness, gather
immensity into my eyes, as if to sing distinct notes
of flame, each body built new.

Kepler's Supernova Remnant

Maybe the remnant tells the whole
story. Maybe the shattering says the one-

ing and we just can't see the we
in its visible form, the unleashed dazzle of matter

not debris but a new creation, what remains
—our cinders, come together—

burning through time and space:
complete, even as the fusion

rives and gnarls the universe and appears
to be expulsion from self. The astronomers trace

the cataclysmic losing of matter into space, knot
by knot, body by body and we know something

about vast collapse that ignites expansion
even here, even in the fragile

mass of the animal heart, which must
                              fissure in order to love.

Eagle Nebula

Perfect capture eludes the usual
techniques. The darkness of outstretched shoulders

feathers the negative space with silhouette
of who you might have been,

while the beak obstinately tilts,
triangulates to the wringing cloud of protostars.

You've tried lens and filter to blot the brightness,
bring up the contrast, penetrate the gloom.

Even so the stellar spires evade you
with smoky green overexposure, soap-bubble stars.

She came for you but the transparency failed. Now
you can only long for her, the eagle arching

across the cosmos. Too brilliant, too obscure to seize
in time.   Hawk over the ridge,

moon below horizon, milky tresses dropped down
out of your reach. This happens

too often. This happens your whole life.
But this time, by damage or design, the image wedges

aquamarine. This time, the leaking light
converts to nebular glow and wing. The decay

slumps, not yours to carry. This time the seeping
salvages the splendor, your swimming flight reversed.

Strawberry Supermoon

Orbits have pulled us
to this moment. Blessed are you
who call me out of darkness to feed me
low-hanging light, waxed amber
and plump. Let this sky-heart grow, summit
at solstice. Let the tongue loll, hunger heighten,
howl. Let the longed-for ripeness come
from night. Your tender words seed, sprout
and stem, widen white-green hips. Only you
write each tender phase copper-pink, hints
of fire. For the first time horizon
and lantern align. The moth careens
into the burn
of her love, and lives—and I can't wrench my eyes
from your brightness, can't tear circumference
from sweetness, can only smolder the plum night
in full.

Hours

1.

You rouse me with gentle blue of the half-moon
window, part the indigo drapes of longing
with love. You have bloomed in the bell of me
the entire night; you touch my cheek with dawn,
light the wick of me awake.

2.

I wash the cup, watching the redtail loop
the sky, waiting for me, calling my eyes to come
rest on the wet green-leaved acacia frond in its talons—
a glinting diamond promise in the morning sun.
And I, like Noah, am split open by a sprig.

3.

Noon should blind me. It should scorch the center
clean. But you, tender, swathe yourself in nimbus gray,
and wild lupines on the muddy trail catch pale rays
in purple lanterns. The fire so quiet—with one petal
you gather me into amethyst flame.

4.

In the afternoon you spatter cloud into light,
bend the brightness vibrant, and I can decipher
your vow: an end to flood, a beginning. The wind whips
a psalm on lute of pine and palm; I accompany, joyful
on harp of lashing hair and tears.

5.
Evening slants pink across foothills as dusk descends
on the sharp-shinned hawk's last flash of white—and I
feel you skim the moon, beloved. Your shine opens
the Casablanca lily of me, at the center the name
that sings in me all night.

Heart as Honeycomb

The Bridegroom says to the Bride, "Your heart has become a
honeycomb full of every kind of instruction."
—GREGORY OF NYSSA

Australian stingless bees aim
their egg nurseries upward

in a spiral,
the same configuration

as crystals grow
their glow   and luminous mother

of pearl multiplies in the mouth
of mollusk.   Sweet sugarbag

bee helix   of beeswax—
trace   of divine finger

in the genes   in the wax,
refraction of gem   glimmer

of pearl   pulsing architectural
evidence

of love   of algorithm
secreted in buzzing cells

which build and bend twenty
terraces high. You who number

the stars, yellow the corners
and planes, bundle the efficient

hexagon—:   you know
the precise sum of tiny wings

you've folded inside
this humming honeycomb,

                    reaching up to you.

Trembling Aspen: Stitch

Can these bones come to life?
—EZEKIEL 37:3

The blow struck, feral, serrated.
Our skulls and spines picked clean, flung
apart, desiccated bones over the plain,
an empty sowing, dry even of lament.
What knits newness from death? Or has pity.
Or strikes lightning. What wields the rejoining
needle, the healing thread? The stripped want,
tattered beggar has been taken in at last.
Some word jolts into guttural prophecy, casts
a net of silvered life, tiny gathering shoots.
We see the infinitesimal weave, never the hand.
Sinew to bone, bone to bone—bone of my bone, flesh
of my flesh—a body assembling out of the topsoil.
A rib, shared. Unseen fingers stitch us into shim-
mering cities, make of us a home. Heart of my heart,
heart-round aspen leaves quiver and quicken
as the spirit blows in, I, dear belly of your belly,
you, belly of me, trunk tinged chlorophyll green,
rising almost imperceptibly.

Stingray Nebula

There is a bitterness edging the blue in the older ones
with cracked, scratched hides. Roughened by risk,
they wear and war with their own cosmic weakness.
They are engineered for hiding—periscope eyes,
silent spiracles. The hunger settles beneath a thin layer
of agitated ocean sediment. They wait in the whims
between teeth. Between *I never should have*
and *I should have*. They know the sting both ways.
There is a relief in the riptide, the steady unsounded
whiptail. It carries like light, limitless through the wring
and weave of wave. Oh beloved thinnest ray, penetrate
without pain. Outstretched pectorals, expanding black holes,
stud and shudder the measureless fabric. Blinding star,
dark nova remnant—overshadow me, hold me in my fading.
Here is the smallest of your infinite galaxies, my atoms,
arrowing to you. Swim me, pull me into the purple deep.
The sheath of body a vast rippling muscle.
A constant becoming.

Keyhole Nebula

opening   in the southern sky   my shard
   to your shard   my rift   your inverse

fitted   we were shattered just so   darkly
   a mirror   in mirror   I knew the hawk

behind me   because I saw the talons in you   rush
   flat flash across the pane   dusky figure eight

nebula cut precise   coring of apple   a bashful
   unfastening   you were always

the grooves in me   even before I knew you,   turning
   the unbolting no one sees

so many keys I was given in the dream   to bestow
   to stow   in the rusted screen door

warped side door   sticking steel lockbox inside   inside
   the clouds blot the shallow pool of window

just the littlest trick to tumble   the cylinders
   slightest click   twist of crisp light

Kilonova as Composition

That he might create in himself one new
person in place of the two, establishing peace.
—EPHESIANS 2:15

Always we listen for the lyric—
the juddering   across space-time.

In the absence of visible lines
of light,   gravitational waves

pull   squeeze
     stretch.

The interferometer detects a collision
of two neutron stars   the merger

jolts   through the cosmos,
tenses shortening tether.

Each star crams
the mass of the sun into a city-sized

home.
An enormity never before observed.

We are listening.   Scientists will study
this   but we hear it now,

the nascent unity   inscribed
in the interstellar chord.

I rotate my body toward the distant hum
of us

together.

Persephone at the Turn

On the night of the longest lunar eclipse in five hundred
years, I was the bright skin of the moon

      passing into ruddy
darkness with my handful of torn poppies. The vast
slung undergarment of the abyss bled across
my scuffed countenance

      leaving only a sliver
of my former self. Then I knew how help flies
before us, tips the bowl of new life

      as we move,
decants the courage of ripened fruit. What came before
crosses into after, the shock of a new shape sliding
over the brim. I have focused

      on the rusted shell
when the trajectory is the pale slip of mist, a swelling
trust in the reversal of night. This morning,

      the road eclipsed
in dense marine layer, yellow painted lines
and reflective markers

      emerge in the headlights
just in time, gleaming constellations that spur me
to keep driving over the miles,

      to lean into the silver
thread widening before me, the knot of pomegranate
slowly broken by light, sowing rubies into spring.

Blue Moon Butterfly

Let me see the wick of wing, white moons
surrounded

by blue-violet halos, etching
the black. Let me remember

it is also not that. Let me be
the compound eye
which slivers
            the ultraviolet spectrum,
populates the invisible

we call hope, which is also
not that. When will you come, Lord?
We have asked over the ages, over

the surfaces that trick light, over structures
that overlay all. Iridescent eyespots

blue the moon, shiver the signal—
your touch tender, silver-bloomed,
lapis ripe—when

you come, Lord, there is no when,
only a different light.
Let me not forget.

ACKNOWLEDGMENTS

Grateful acknowledgment is made to the editors of the following publications in which some of these poems first appeared, sometimes in a slightly different form:

America Magazine: The Jesuit Review of Faith & Culture, "St. Teresa's Pillow" and "Coalsack Nebula"

Amethyst, "Ribbons"

Amsterdam Quarterly, "A Small Good Friday Service at Notre Dame Cathedral"

Another Chicago Magazine, "Kepler's Supernova Remnant" and "Longing as Dark Matter"

Beyond the Frame (Diode Editions, 2023), "Eagle Nebula" and "Heart Nebula"

The Christian Century, "Blue Moon Butterfly"

Cider Press Review, "Resilience as Daffodil"

Cloudbank, "Twine" and "Stitch" (now titled "Trembling Aspen: Twine" and "Trembling Aspen: Stitch")

Connecticut River Review, "Persephone at the Turn"

DMQ Review, "Needle" (now titled "Trembling Aspen: Needle")

EcoTheo Review, "Sign of the Times"

Eye to the Telescope, "Psyche as Vampire Squid"

The Inflectionist Review, "Prayer for Traversing the Eye"

LETTERS Journal, "Kilonova as Composition" and "Your Never and Always Ring of Fire"

Lily Poetry Review, "Heart as Siphonophore"

Mantis, "Sea Butterfly" and "Question Mark Butterfly"

McMaster Journal of Theology and Ministry, "Exchange" and "Soul as Half Moon"

The Night Heron Barks, "The Mother Gives Us"

Pensive: A Global Journal of Spirituality and the Arts, "Via Negativa: New Moon"

Poetry International Online, "Petri Dish"

Presence: A Journal of Catholic Poetry, "Fast Radio Bursts Detected Close to Earth"

Psaltery & Lyre, "The Elysia Sea Slug"

Reformed Journal, "Letter" and "Strawberry Supermoon"

Relief: A Journal of Art and Faith, "Mary, Wife of Clopas" and "Via Negativa: Corpse Flower"

RHINO, "Butterfly Nebula"

River Heron Review, "HR 6819 and the Lovesick Be Star"

Rock & Sling, "Iris Nebula" and "Lazarus Rising"

Rust + Moth, "Playing with Tiger Sharks on the Missile Range"

Scientific American, "Lyrebird"

Sojourners, "Ghost Nebula"

Solum Journal, "Geminids," "Hope as Alpha Centauri AB," and "Soul Nebula"

Spiritus, "Fireball"

Sugar House Review, "Between 50 and 51"

SWWIM *Every Day*, "Manatee Nebula"

Trinity House Review, "Heart as Honeycomb"

U.S. Catholic, "Bow in the Clouds"

Vassar Review, "Keyhole Nebula"

The Windhover, "Comma Butterfly," "Oyster Nebula," and "Petition as Praying Mantis"

Without a Doubt (New York Quarterly, 2023), "Moon Rust"

"Fast Radio Bursts Detected Close to Earth" also appeared in *Verse Daily*.

I am tremendously grateful to Christine Stewart-Nuñez for selecting this book as the winner of the 2022 Backwaters Prize in Poetry.

Thank you to Nan Cohen and Donna Spruijt-Metz for their readings and improvements of many of these poems, and their loving support. Thank you to Elizabeth Kuelbs, David Keplinger, and Lisa Smith for invaluable wisdom and encouragement, each in their various ways.

Seas and skies of thanks to my children, Caitlin, Connor, and Amanda, for sharing their scientific curiosity and wonder with me.

I am grateful to all who have given me their kindness and support, especially Mark Wunderlich, Dana Gioia, D. S. Martin, John Sibley Williams, Jane Hirshfield, Gillian Conoley, Dana Levin, Mark S. Burrows, Paul J. Willis, Craig Morgan Teicher, Suzanne Underwood Rhodes, Sofia Starnes, Sarah Law, Matthew Wickman, Br. Joe Hoover, SJ, Luke Hankins, Shann Ray, Susan Rose, Jill Peláez Baumgaertner, Mary Ann Miller, Marjorie Maddox, Lois Roma-Deeley, J. P. Dancing Bear, Eileen Cleary, Josiah A. R. Cox, Riley Bounds, Rose Berger, Dava Sobel, Nathaniel Lee Hansen, Jeffrey Essmann, Tim Bete, Ray Waddle, Rose Postma, Jody Collins, Michael J. Gorman, Brian Volck, Lesley Clinton, Jason Gray, Christal Rice Cooper, Tania Runyan, Sally Thomas, Mischa Willett, Elline Lipkin, Flower Conroy, Phil Taggart, Marsha de la O, Bonnie Naradzay, Caroline Barnes, Ann Quinn, Jeremy Proehl, Michael Battisto, Joel Katz, Moriah Cohen, Fr. Nicholas Blackwell, OCarm, Fr. Steven Payne, OCD, Br. Daryl Moresco, OCarm, Sr. Mary Grace Melcher, OCD, and Sr. Mary Clare Mancini, OCD.

Thank you to the Bread Loaf Writers' Conference, especially Jennifer Grotz, Noreen Cargill, Jason Lamb, and Lauren Francis-Sharma, and to the Napa Valley Writers' Conference, especially Angela Pneuman, Andrea Bewick, Iris Dunkle, and Nan Cohen.

I am deeply grateful to the Backwaters Press, the University of Nebraska Press, and particularly Emily Casillas, Haley Mendlik, Rosemary Sekora, Tish Fobben, Tayler Lord, and Leif Milliken.

To friends, my Lay Carmelite community, and my family, my enduring gratitude and love.

The Backwaters Prize in Poetry was suspended from 2005 to 2011.

To order or obtain more information on these or other University of Nebraska Press titles, visit nebraskapress.unl.edu.

9 781496 236104